Wizard Laughs and Riddles

300+ Potterverse Jokes & Riddles

This book belongs to:

____

____

ABOUT KODE SCRIPT

Welcome to Kode Script, a dynamic publishing company dedicated to crafting digital stories with precision.

At Kode Script, we believe in the transformative power of creativity and education. Specializing in a diverse range of publications, from enchanting coloring books that spark imagination to mind-teasing riddles and puzzles for all ages, we cater to children, adults, and senior individuals alike.

Our mission is to seamlessly blend entertainment with learning, providing enriching experiences through meticulously designed content. With a commitment to quality and innovation, Kode Script invites you to embark on a journey where every page tells a story and every puzzle unveils a new adventure.

If you like our books, please provide your positive reviews on Amazon or any other marketplace. your support will motivate us to do better.

 **email : info@kodescript.com**  **www.kodescript.com**

COPYRIGHT© 2024 BY KODE SCRIPT
ALL RIGHTS RESERVED

Why did Harry bring a ladder to Quidditch practice?

Because he wanted to reach new heights!

What's a Death Eater's favorite snack

Slytherin rolls.

Why doesn't Voldemort use social media?

He can't handle followers.

Why did Hermione never get lost?
Because she had a "book" for every situation.

What do you call a Hufflepuff who becomes a ghost?
A Puff-pastry.

Why don't they let Slytherins into the kitchen?
They're always cooking up trouble.

Why did Ron blush when he saw a spell book?

He thought it was a "Charm" book.

What spell does Harry use to fix his glasses?

Optomendious!

Why did Voldemort cross the road?

To avoid Dumbledore on the other side.

What's a wizard's favorite cereal?

CheeriOwls.

What's Draco's favorite type of music?

Slytherin rap.

Why did Hagrid bring a ruler to the Forbidden Forest?

To measure up to the centaurs.

What does Hermione say when she
runs out of books?
"This is riddikulus!"

Why did the wand get detention?
It was being too "pointy."

What's a house-elf's favorite sport?
Quid-ditch.

Why didn't the basilisk go to school?

It was petrified of homework.

What's a wizard's favorite exercise?

Dumble-doors.

Why did Harry's wand get a promotion?

It was outstanding in its field.

Why don't muggles play Quidditch?
They can't handle the broom traffic.

What's Voldemort's favorite kind of weather?
Foggy — because it's "no-sunny."

Why did Snape open a bakery?
To make potion cakes.

What do you call a magical fish?
A Hufflepuffin!

Why is Dobby bad at hide-and-seek?
He always elf-reveals himself.

What's a wizard's favorite type of tea?
Spell-o-mint.

Why did the Gryffindor start a band?
Because they wanted to be roaring success.

Why did the Sorting Hat start a blog?
To share its "thoughts."

What's the most magical type of clothing?
Hocus-pockets.

What do you call a wizard who's great at bowling?

Lord Spare-emort.

Why was Ron afraid of the chessboard?

He didn't want to get knighted.

Why don't dementors ever get invited to parties?

They're a bit of a "soul sucker."

What does a Slytherin say during exams?

"Let's snake through this."

Why did the broom refuse to fly?

It was swept off its feet.

What's Harry's favorite breed of dog?

The Hagrid-doodle.

Why didn't Harry go skydiving?

He was afraid of "falling for Voldemort."

What's the best way to break into Hogwarts?

Through the Dumbled-doors.

What do you call a magical owl who loves math?

Owlgebra.

Why was Dobby bad at jokes?

Because he was too literal — "Dobby has no pun, sir."

What's a wizard's favorite game?

Spelliards.

Why didn't the potion master play cards?

He didn't trust the "deck."

Why did Voldemort become a vegetarian?

Because meat is "Horcruxing" his health.

What's a wizard's favorite candy?

Fizzy Wizzbees.

Why does Hagrid never lose at chess?

He's got giant moves.

What's Draco's favorite board game?
Snakes and Ladders.

Why did Hermione become a great cook?
She always followed the "recipe for success."

What's a magical cat's favorite spell?
Furr-finitum!

Why don't goblins play soccer?
They're afraid of losing their "goal-d."

What's Ron's favorite kind of juice?
Pumpkin spice!

Why did the broom break up with the mop?
Because it was swept away by the dustpan.

What's Snape's favorite type of bread?

Slytherin sourdough.

Why did Harry avoid the fortune teller?

He didn't want "grim news."

Why did the snitch go to therapy?

It had too many unresolved issues.

What's a wizard's favorite instrument?
The magical harp-string.

Why doesn't Voldemort like puns?
Because he's a little "no-nonsense."

What's a Hogwarts student's favorite game console?
The Hexbox.

Why did the cauldron fail its exam?

It cracked under pressure.

What's Draco's favorite snack?

Malfoy-sticks.

Why did Luna open a zoo?

She wanted to prove Nargles are real.

What's a Slytherin's favorite type of bread?
Sneaky buns.

Why did Dumbledore start gardening?
To grow a new kind of magic herb.

Why was Ron bad at painting?
He always ran out of "brushes" with greatness.

What's a wizard's favorite type of drink?

Butterbeer floats!

Why was Hagrid a great chef?

He always added a "giant" pinch of salt.

What's a magical car's favorite music genre?

Auto-tunes.

Why did Hermione win the race?
Because she knew all the shortcuts.

What's Voldemort's favorite hobby?
Horcrux collecting.

Why did Neville bring soil to the library?
He wanted to plant himself in a good book.

What spell fixes bad jokes?
Riddikulus!

Why did the Gryffindor knight retire?
Because he ran out of brave ideas.

What's a wizard's favorite dessert?
Spell-tarts.

Why was Snape always angry?
He never found his "Potion of Chill."

What's a ghost's favorite spell?
Apparition.

Why do wizards love breakfast?
Because it's a magical start to their day.

What's Voldemort's least favorite part
of Halloween?
The masks.

Why was the wand so successful?
Because it had a strong "point."

What's Hermione's favorite app?
Spell-check.

Why don't Death Eaters eat pizza?
They're afraid of getting sliced.

What do you call a magical diary?
Tom's Secret Keeper.

Why didn't the wizard get a haircut?
Because it was a hairy situation.

What's a witch's favorite accessory?

A spell-ed bracelet.

Why don't Slytherins play hide-and-seek?

They're too good at sneaking.

What's Harry's favorite spell for cleaning?

Scourgify!

Why did the wand get grounded?
It cast a rebellious spell.

What's a wizard's favorite camping gear?
A magical tent.

Why did Ron avoid the dentist?
Because he feared the molar monster.

Why do wizards avoid thunderstorms?
They might lose their spark.

What's a Quidditch team's favorite fruit?
Bludger-berries.

Why didn't the basilisk join the track team?
It was a little "stiff."

What's a wizard's favorite app?

Snapchat (Snape-chat)!

Why did Voldemort open a bakery?

He wanted to make dark chocolate cookies.

What's the Marauder's Map's favorite drink?

Espresso — it always knows where you're going.

Why was the broom so tired?

It swept through the entire day.

What's Draco's favorite drink?

Mal-tea.

Why did Harry's glasses break?

Because they were hexed!

What's a wizard's favorite way to relax?

By casting a Chill-axio spell.

Why did Hermione start a bookstore?

Because she knew how to "spell" success.

What's a wizard's favorite workout?

Quid-ditch jumping.

Why do Slytherins love riddles?
They enjoy twisting words.

Why did Ron wear earmuffs?
To keep the howlers out.

What do you call a witch who's great at math?
An Arithmancy wizard.

Why didn't Harry play hide and seek with Ron?

Because the Cloak of Invisibility made it unfair.

What do you call a magical snake with great manners?

A civil Serpent.

Why does Voldemort never take holidays?

Because he's afraid of losing "control" of his Horcruxes.

What's Hermione's favorite holiday?

Booktoberfest.

Why did Luna bring a ladder to class?

To reach her lofty ideas.

What's a wizard's favorite way to
watch movies?

Spell-vision.

Why didn't Snape join the Quidditch team?

He didn't want to play "keeper" to anyone else.

Why do Gryffindors never gossip?

Because they're too brave to spread rumors.

What do you call a wizard who loves sandwiches?

A Gryffin-deli.

Why did Hagrid open a gym?

To teach people how to "lift like a giant."

What's Voldemort's favorite board game?

Risk — he likes taking over territories.

Why did the sorting hat take a day off?

It needed to "re-think" things.

What do you call a Hufflepuff at a party?
The life of the pumpkin juice keg.

Why did the wand get promoted?
It made magical "points" during the meeting.

What's Harry's favorite type of joke?
Ones with "Potter-y" punchlines.

Why did Draco bring an umbrella?

To protect himself from charm storms.

What's a wizard's favorite animal?

A Hippogriff — because it's "Griffin" awesome.

Why did the Quidditch team get new brooms?

The old ones were sweeping the competition!

What's a wizard's favorite plant?
Mandrake-shakes.

Why don't wizards play chess with muggles?
Because their pieces always move magically.

What do you call a magical nap?
A spell-slumber.

Why was Ron's wand acting up?

It was feeling a bit "wooden."

What's Dumbledore's favorite music genre?

Classic alchemy.

Why did the Gryffindor take a cooking class?

To learn how to make "bold flavors."

What's a Slytherin's favorite movie?

The Serpent's Tale.

Why was the golden snitch nervous?

It didn't want to be caught off-guard.

What's Hermione's favorite type of math?

Wizard-ometry.

Why did the broomstick go to school?
To brush up on its skills.

What's Harry's favorite mode of transportation?
The Floo Network — it's lit!

Why didn't Voldemort use a GPS?
He liked leaving a dark trail.

What's a Hufflepuff's favorite game?
Badger Ball.

Why was the Forbidden Forest always
so noisy?
Because of the centaur of attention.

What do you call a wizard in a hurry?
A speed-caster.

Why did Hermione knit so many hats?
Because she wanted Dobby to "captivate" freedom.

What's Snape's favorite joke?
"Why so Sirius?"

Why don't wizards do laundry?
Because they just charm their clothes clean.

What's Voldemort's least favorite
spell?
Happify!

Why did the wand go to therapy?
**It couldn't handle the pressure of
casting spells.**

What's Draco's favorite spell for
dating?
Charm-io!

Why did the cauldron get an award?
For being stirringly good.

What's a wizard's favorite app for delivery?
Hexpress Eats.

Why did the owl refuse to carry mail?
It wanted to "wing" its own business.

What's Harry's favorite TV show?
The Great British Spell-Off.

Why do Slytherins love working out?
To stay sneaky strong.

What's Hagrid's least favorite spell?
Shrinko-maximus.

Why did the wand lose its job?

It was fired for misconducting magic.

What's a magical prankster's favorite dessert?

Jelly beans with hex flavoring.

Why doesn't Voldemort like to dance?

Because he has two left feet.

What's Hermione's favorite holiday treat?
Ginger wand cookies.

Why did Ron bring a ruler to Quidditch?
To measure his success.

Why didn't the Slytherin bring a map?
Because they already know all the shortcuts.

What's Harry's favorite pastry?

Dumble-doughnuts.

Why did the broomstick start a business?

It wanted to sweep the market.

What do you call a magical vegetable?

A spell-cumber.

Why don't wizards use telephones?
They prefer spell-egrams.

What's a Ravenclaw's favorite type of music?
Enchanted jazz.

Why did the cauldron become a motivational speaker?
It's great at stirring up emotions.

What's a wizard's favorite exercise equipment?
Dumb-bellatrix.

Why was the snitch so popular?
Because it always had people chasing after it.

What do you call a wizard who's bad at directions?
Lost-a-lot.

Why did Ron eat so much candy?
To sweeten up his chances with Hermione.

What's Voldemort's favorite hobby?
Dark arts and crafts.

Why did Harry bring sunscreen to the Forbidden Forest?
He heard there were shady characters.

What do you call a magical fruit?
Hocus-pocus-berry.

Why didn't the Dementor go to the party?
It didn't want to suck the fun out of the room.

What's a wizard's favorite fast food?
Charmed fries.

Why did Hermione start a tutoring club?

To charm her way into helping others.

What do you call a magical musician?

A wand-tar player.

Why did Hagrid buy a new chair?

The old one couldn't handle his giant personality.

What's a wizard's favorite flower?
Snap-dragons.

Why don't wizards go camping?
They hate tent-sion.

What do you call a magical
sandwich?
A spell-wich.

Why did Harry avoid the Marauder's Map one day?
He didn't want to be followed.

What's a wizard's favorite subject?
Spell-ing.

Why did the wand start a podcast?
It wanted to cast its voice far and wide.

Why was Voldemort bad at hide-and-seek?

He was too nosey.

What's Hermione's favorite type of pizza?

Cheesy charms.

Why did the Quidditch player refuse to play cards?

Because they didn't want to deal.

What's a wizard's favorite sport?
Spellminton.

Why did the owl become a teacher?
It always had "wise" words to share.

What's a wizard's favorite fruit?
Spell-peaches.

Why did Ron fail Potions class?

Because he stirred things up too late.

What's a Slytherin's favorite vacation spot?

Snake Island.

Why did Harry go to the bakery?

To find some dough for his adventures.

What's a magical camera called?
A Snaparazzi.

Why don't wizards ride bicycles?
They prefer broomsticks — no wheels required.

What's Hagrid's favorite song?
"I'm a Believer" (in giants).

Why was the Sorting Hat so good at guessing?

It always had the inside scoop.

What's a wizard's favorite TV show?

Hexflix Originals.

Why did the wand write a novel?

It wanted to craft a spell-binding tale.

What's a wizard's favorite drink?
Potion soda.

Why did Hermione start a book club?
Because knowledge is magic.

What do you call a magical train?
A spell-express.

Why did the snitch need a nap?

It was tired of flying in circles.

What's Voldemort's least favorite dessert?

Pumpkin pie — it's too Gryffindor-ish.

Why do wizards hate bad weather?

It messes with their broomstick steering.

What's a Ravenclaw's favorite game?
Trivia spells.

Why did Ron avoid the potion contest?
He didn't want to get into hot water.

What's Harry's favorite day of the week?
Wizard Wednesday.

Why don't wizards play Monopoly?
They already have all the magic money.

Why did the cauldron take a vacation?
It was tired of being stirred up.

What's a wizard's favorite board game?
Spell-nopoly.

Why did the broomstick break up with the wand?

They swept in different directions.

What's a wizard's favorite type of bread?

Enchanted sourdough.

Why did Ron bring a compass to Potions class?

To find his way out of trouble.

What do you call a witch who likes to garden?
A spell-flower.

Why did the Quidditch team bring snacks?
To keep their energy flying high.

What's Hermione's favorite dessert?
Magical macaroons.

Why don't wizards use the internet?
They prefer spell-servers.

What's a wizard's favorite workout?
Casting reps.

Why did the golden snitch take a break?
It was feeling flighty.

What's Voldemort's favorite movie?

The Dark Knight.

Why did Harry fail his Herbology test?

He didn't have time to "root" for success.

What's a wizard's favorite cake?

Spell-berry shortcake.

Why did Hagrid bring a broom to class?

He wanted to sweep the floor with the competition.

What's a Slytherin's favorite vegetable?

Sneaky peas.

Why don't wizards play basketball?

Because they always foul up their spells.

What's a wizard's favorite sandwich topping?
Spell-tuna.

Why did the wand go on strike?
It was tired of being used.

What's a wizard's favorite movie genre?
Magical realism.

Why did the Quidditch team throw a party?

To celebrate their sweeping success.

What's Hermione's least favorite spell?

Forget-io.

Why did Ron bring a camera to class?

To capture magical moments.

What's Voldemort's least favorite fruit?

Harry-berries.

Why did Harry bring a magnifying glass to Quidditch?

To spot the snitch more easily.

What do you call a magical owl who loves history?

Hist-o-hoot.

Why was the wand jealous of the broomstick?

Because it had all the sweeping success.

What's Hagrid's favorite sport?

Rugby — giants love a good tackle.

Why did the potion explode?

It had too much pressure to perform.

What's a wizard's favorite fruit?

Spell-apples.

Why did Luna Lovegood start a podcast?

To share her loony theories.

What's a wizard's least favorite math class?

Arithmancy miscalculations.

Why did Harry love the library?

Because it always had magical "volumes."

What's a wizard's favorite fast-food chain?

Magic McSpells.

Why don't wizards play video games?

They prefer spell simulators.

What's Voldemort's favorite candy?

Dark chocolate frogs.

Why did Ron get a broom for his birthday?

To sweep into Quidditch fame.

What's a wizard's favorite card game?

Spell Poker.

Why don't Dementors like jokes?
They suck the fun out of everything.

What's Hermione's favorite type of tea?
Chamomile charm.

Why did the Sorting Hat start a vlog?
To share its top hat picks.

What's a wizard's favorite pet?
A spell-canine.

Why did the wand refuse to duel?
It didn't want to "stick" to violence.

What's Hagrid's favorite drink?
Butter-beer floats.

Why did Harry practice with a mirror?
To reflect on his spells.

What's a wizard's favorite breakfast?
Magic muffins.

Why did the broomstick join a club?
To sweep up new friends.

What's a Slytherin's favorite ice cream flavor?

Snakeberry.

Why did Hermione write a cookbook?

To create charming recipes.

What's Harry's least favorite candy?

Licorice wands — too chewy.

Why didn't the cauldron win the race?

It couldn't handle the pressure.

What's a wizard's favorite smartphone feature?

Spell-check, of course!

Why did the Quidditch team avoid playing at night?

Because they didn't want to be caught in a "dark arts storm."

What's Hagrid's least favorite spell?

Shrinkify — it cramps his style.

Why did Ron bring a ladder to Potions class?

To reach new heights of potion-making.

What's a wizard's favorite vacation spot?

Magic Mountain.

Why did the wand become an artist?
Because it loved making magical strokes.

What's a wizard's favorite snack?
Hex-mix.

Why did the Sorting Hat get stuck?
It couldn't make up its mind!

What's Voldemort's favorite style of architecture?

Dark Gothic.

Why did Harry avoid eating at the Great Hall?

He didn't want a "charmed meal."

What's a wizard's favorite type of dance?

Spell-ettos.

Why don't wizards wear sunglasses?
They use Lumos to see the light.

What's Hermione's least favorite joke?
One without a good point — she's all about structure.

Why did the owl always deliver mail on time?
It had impeccable wing-management.

What's Draco's least favorite class?
Care of Magical Creatures — too messy for his taste.

Why did Ron carry a backpack full of candy?
To always have a sweet escape.

What's a wizard's favorite pizza topping?
Spell-pepperoni.

Why did the cauldron join the debate club?

It loved stirring up discussions.

What's Harry's favorite magical sport besides Quidditch?

Wizard Ping-Pong.

Why did Voldemort refuse a haircut?

Because he liked looking sharp.

What's a wizard's favorite vegetable?
Carrots of the magical kind.

Why was the broom always happy?
It loved flying high above its problems.

What do you call a wizard's favorite party game?
Pin the wand on the wizard.

Why did the Sorting Hat go to therapy?

It had too many unresolved "house" issues.

What's a wizard's favorite condiment?

Magical mustard.

Why did Ron keep his wand in his pocket?

So he could always have a "pocket full of spells."

What's a wizard's favorite type of weather?

A light magical drizzle.

Why didn't Voldemort play football?

He wasn't a "goal" oriented person.

What's Hagrid's favorite Quidditch position?

Keeper — because he's great at protecting things.

Why did Harry love magic mirrors?

They always reflected well on him.

What's a wizard's favorite soup?

Spell-minestrone.

Why did Hermione never lose at trivia?

Because she was a master of magical facts.

What's a wizard's favorite season?
Fall — when the leaves start to enchant.

Why don't wizards need flashlights?
They always have Lumos.

What's a wizard's favorite type of shoe?
Spell-sandals.

Why did the wand go to school?
To learn how to spell better.

What's a wizard's favorite type of jewelry?
Enchanted charms.

Why did Ron bring a watch to Quidditch practice?
To keep an eye on "overtime."

What's a wizard's favorite card game?

Magic: The Gathering.

Why did the golden snitch win the talent show?

Because it was always on point.

What's a wizard's least favorite chore?

Sweeping — ironic for broomsticks!

Why did Voldemort avoid public speaking?
Because he didn't have a nose for it.

What's Hermione's favorite flower?
Spell-roses.

Why did the owl fail its exam?
It winged it without studying.

What's a wizard's favorite type of car?

A flying Ford Anglia.

Why did the broomstick apply for a new job?

It wanted a sweeping career change.

What's a wizard's favorite kind of cookie?

Spell-chip cookies.

Why did the cauldron get a promotion?

Because it was always brewing up good ideas.

What's Hagrid's favorite pie?

Giant berry pie.

Why did the Slytherin fail Potions?

They were too "snake-y" with their measurements.

What's a wizard's favorite coffee order?
Cappu-charm-o.

Why did the wand love the library?
It was full of spell-binding tales.

What's Voldemort's favorite holiday?
Halloween — it's all about darkness and magic.

Why did Ron open a bakery?
To make magical treats.

What's Harry's favorite hobby?
Collecting magical memorabilia.

Why did the Quidditch team buy umbrellas?
To avoid rain delays.

What's a wizard's least favorite fruit?

Bad apples — they don't charm anyone.

Why did the Sorting Hat love karaoke?

It always hit the right notes.

What's Hagrid's favorite cake?

Rock cakes — literally.

Why did Hermione ace her Arithmancy test?

She calculated every possibility.

What's a wizard's favorite drink at Starbucks?

It always hit the right notes.

Why did Voldemort open a clothing line?

To create a new line of dark robes.

What's Ron's favorite spell?
Expelliarmus — it saves him every time.

Why do wizards love libraries?
Because they're full of magical volumes.

What's a wizard's favorite ice cream?
Spell-mint chip.

Why don't wizards need alarm clocks?

They just cast "Wake-up-io!"

What's a wizard's favorite spell for relaxation?

Chillio Maximus!

What's Hagrid's favorite bedtime story?

Anything about giants, of course.

Why did the wand refuse to duel?

It didn't want to break under pressure.

THANK YOU!